The Pros and Cons 4 a Singled Man

My singled history

I have been singled practically my whole life. Even though I have dated a few women, I still have been singled. If you have to use a condom during your relationship, it means you are still single because condoms are for fuck buddies. When I was like 14 I used to be happy as hell going to the store to get a condom to show people how grown I was. Now going to the store asking for condoms at the age of 30 is now embarrassing because it was telling people that I was either single or cheating on my significant other. Condoms are meant for safe sex between partners not in a relationship but only for fuck buddies and one night stands. And it shames me that I have used condoms 95% of the times during sexual intercourse in my whole life which tells you how long I have been singled and how many risks I have done took. I have gotten so used to wearing hats, that when I tried to go in naked, I bust within two minutes. That's the downfall about being single for too long because the longer you wear condoms the shorter time you last in the punani. Well, the bright side of being single is that you'll be able to focus on your goals without being distracted. Even the female friends I dealt with were a big distraction and we weren't in any relationship, so I imagined where I would be if I stayed in a long-term relationship. We men have to remember that women need time more than anything else. Money, jewelry, sex may temporary satisfy them but spending quality time with them is really all what they want. I was too busy I couldn't give that type of attention to women. That's why I was singled my whole life because I thought of my goals being more important than spending time with my woman. I did not look at women as a cheap asset; instead I have always respected them. I just wasn't ready for commitment. I have grew up in a household full of women because of the absent of my father; so you know I have major respect for women. That was another downfall because when my mother taught me how to treat women, I have been too nice to women which kept me single. Being picky and too nice kept me out of relationships. I learned later in my life that woman likes to be disrespected, miss treated and bossed around sometimes because they think if a man can't control her he can't protect her. That's how they test a man by starting an argument to see will he take his stand or be too

6

nice. There's nothing wrong with being nice, but being too nice is annoying most of the time to them. That's why I was kicked to the curve without any explanation because they didn't think I can protect them no matter how big my muscles were. This is the main reason why a lot of good men are single. My theory is that the reason why many good men are singled is because there aren't many good women left to appreciate that quality in a man. We are dealing with the second millennium women who has a personality way different from the 80s women.

I can't really speak on why single women are singled. All I can think is that they been through the bullshit already. But many are because they are stuck up, conceited (which is a turn off to men) or high classed which makes underachieved men feel inferior around their success. Women with money will stay singled longer than men with money because a man is supposed to take care of his woman. A man won't feel like a man being taken care of by his woman. That's the way He designed us. We men are equipped with this thing called EGO, while women are showered with insecurity for the purpose of the man to secure them and make them feel comfortable. Women needs constant compliments to feel comfortable in her own skin but there's nothing a person can say to destroy a man's ego unless he's fruity.

The good things about being singled are many. Being single doesn't mean nobody want you, it just means you have more time to grow. You can watch yourself grow up, and growing up individually will make you independent. You shouldn't use your time alone as indication of loneliness but should use that time to learn more about yourself and others too. Being single doesn't mean you need to be in a relationship, it means God is still working on you as an individual, so that when situations get difficult, you'll be able to handle yourself. When people rush into a relationship, they try to rush out of the relationship when they find out that it wasn't right for them. A lot of people are misled by the "love by first sight" thing which makes them believe they are in love after seeing a person for the first time. Then they realize what the heck they were seeing in that person. Truthfully it takes a lifetime with somebody to actually fall in love. Falling in love takes years not days. That "love by first sight" is no more than lust itself. You just want something because it looks good to you at the moment. It should take no more than a month for a person to decide if they want to spend the rest of their life with someone. If you like somebody and want to get in a relationship with that person without first thinking about spending the rest of your life with that person, you've been misled by desire and lust. The only problem I have with being single is I've been single for too long. If you've watched every porn site on the net, it means you've been single too long. If you ran out of all the bottles of lotion, it means you been single for too long. However there are benefits for being single but there is also downfalls being singled. Here are the pros and Cons.

Pros and Cons for being single

PROS: It saves you tons of money (especially holidays). You don't have to lock your phone by putting in a password. You can date different people. If you're a man, you don't have to pay for dinner for two. You don't have to smell bad breath in the morning. If you're a woman, you don't have to iron his clothes before he go to work. If you're a man, you don't have to help her with laundry (such as carrying overloaded laundry bags). If you're a woman, you don't have to hear his friends shout during the football or other sport games. If you're a man, you don't have to sit with her to watch lifetime movies; also you can watch sports in peace. You don't have to worry about her so-called male best friend who she claims she went to high school with.

You don't have to hear those words I'm pregnant! When you're not ready, you can sleep as wide as you want. You are naggy free. You won't see period pads left in a bin in the bathroom. You can leave your phone anywhere in the house. You have more time for yourself. No petty arguments.

CONS: You have to masturbate to kill your sexual desire. You have to spend money to buy condoms. You have to pay for a massage. You have a monthly bill for a dating online website. You eat more fast-food if you can't cook. You can't watch scary movies by yourself (for women). Can't watch romance movies on Netflix. You lose motivation. You feel lonely. You're embarrassed when Valentine's Day comes because you have no one to buy you chocolate or no one you can give a teddy bear to. You have nobody to split the bill when you go out to eat. Your lips are dry all day. Your tub water is colder. You have nobody to show off to your family and friends. Nobody cooks you breakfast. You have nobody to argue with.

The Alternative

When you're looking for sex online:
The infamous Craiglist in the dating
section and Backpage are known for
prostitution better known as
donations. Craiglist is full of
wastetimers and Backpage is a hit or
miss. Actually you're not going to find
what you're looking for on Backpage.
First of all the escorts doesn't do all
the things they promised in their ads.
Their service is so bad you're better
off saving money and masturbate.
Maybe because I only dealt with the
black escorts for the reason being too
afraid to take chances with white

escorts knowing it's a 50-50 chance they could be undercover. I've never trusted the Asian girls too because their profiles always clean and too professional to be real, and some of them share the same numbers which turned me away. I would only pick an Asian girl if she can do an outcall. 99% of the escorts I dealt with all applied rush service to me. Majority of the time they are unorganized by having multiple men come to their room at once. They does this incase a client doesn't show up, they'll have one ready. But if a client shows up who wants to wait outside or who wants to be banging punani then being distracted by knocks on her door. Craiglist! Well Craiglist is a big fail for a dating site. If you're gay then it's not. But as for me, finding a chick to smash on Craiglist was impossible for at least in my area. All the girls that posted an ad on Craiglist were either catfishing or promoters for other dating websites. I got so frustrated trying to find sex on there; I posted my own ad in the W4M section. Unfortunately, I got the wrong kind of replies. I was pretty sure that I posted my ad in the W4M category but somehow when I opened my emails, a lot of gay men (especially old like 40s and 50) offered sex with me and I was shocked not only how many so-called gays replied but how man straight or DLs there were. When I looked at the pics they sent me, a lot of them were straight men that I already knew or seen before that I wouldn't expect to be like that. That confused me because none of them looked gay; they just liked to get duped in the ass. One of them that I knew from work admitted that it's a different experience that offers the same amount of pleasure as the penis, is why he enjoys getting duped. I told him I was glad that it's something I will never get to enjoy. Another dating website I was on that I had to delete my account because of faggots, was tagged. Now tagged is secretly a site for transsexuals and gays. Of all the women I hit up on tagged, none replied or the ones that did were catfishing. The people that offered me sex were all trannies. Before deactivating my account, I have blocked 145 gays and transsexuals. Not that I hate them, I'm just not interested in what they offered me. So I got rid of tagged (transsexual site) Craiglist (gay site) and Backpage (undercover site) and now I am just currently using black people meet. I don't mean to offend anybody sexual orientation, I have amassed amount of respect for gays, transsexuals and DLs but it's not my philosophy. But here's what I think about homosexuality.

Homosexuality

Growing up, I hated gays with a passion. I hated gays like Hitler hated Jews. I didn't really understand why I hated gays so much, I just thought of them as a group of people who are a disgrace to humanity. After studying the bible, I have used the Mosaic Laws to badmouth gays and a reason to exterminate them. Then when I studied the scriptures deeply, I come to realize that I was judging instead of helping. I learned to never judge people but to influence people. I don't think it is fair to judge a person who has become an outlaw to his own body or family; who is desperately looking for help. Homosexuality is more like a transition (that can be a life-time) than a lustful state of mind or trend. Something that's trending doesn't mean it will last. What I mean is sometimes when straight men become gay, they get stuck in homosexuality because there are not much people to help them get out of it. I consider homosexuality as a hacked person, and the reason why they stay like that is because no one to is there to expel the curse out of them. I believe this because in the bible, the prophets were expelling all kinds of demons and curses (including homosexuality) out of sinners. With that being said, homosexuality is a negative state of mind, but doesn't mean the person is sinning all alone, instead he's hacked. This is why it's wrong to hate gays because they are not bad people, they are just transitioning. In fact, with the increasing of homosexuality, I had no choice but to get along with them. Some of them are family members, some are co-workers and some are now friends.

I hesitated to ask questions that people don't ask about homosexuality knowing that the majority part of the world (especially America) embraces it which means I can easily be destroyed. I might be killed, threaten or people will destroy my imaged. That's why if I get too well known I will record myself in every sex act with a woman (if not married) so they won't do me like they did Michael Jackson and Bill Cosby.

This is why I think homosexuality is a not a natural thing. If a gay man is attracted to straight men, and a straight man is attracted to women; how are gay marriages real? Two gay couples are hypocritical, because to be a gay man is to be attracted to men (masculine). But how can a gay man be attracted to another gay man if they both are feminism or view themselves as females. Shouldn't gay men call themselves lesbians since they think they are women? Same as for lesbian women who stick "penis like" objects in their vaginas but they're not attracted to men? And a women attracted to a dike don't know whether she want a man or a woman. My question is, is being homosexual has something to do with being attracted to the same sex or is it a sexual desire? A man that likes being duped; is that his personal sexual preference or is that homosexuality? A woman that likes being licked by another woman; is that's her personal sexual preference or is that being a lesbian? Why does it take 12 years for a boy to decide that he is gay if gay supposed to be natural. Why does it take on an average of 18 years for a woman to say she is a lesbian? Seeing homosexuality during infancy or even early childhood is never seen and that's something nobody wants to talk about. To me it's just a trend to a person who became an outlaw to his own body looking for help. My personal opinion is if a man enjoys another presence of a man before a woman is gay and vice versa. I believe same sex intercourse is more of a sin against God than homosexuality, because homosexuality is a state of mind.

GS7 2000 Fantasy Love Doll

So after I realize that Backpage, Craiglist and Tagged were a waste of time, I went back to Pornhub. For the following year I've purchased myself a $5000 GS7 2000 Fantasy love doll. It was made out of human flesh. It has 5 vibration and humping speeds: slow, fast, medium, slow motion and matrix. It can mimic any celebrity or porn-star moaning vocals when you enter a name in the wireless keypad; which is good for fantasizing. It has a replaceable mouth where you can choose (from the 4 mouth types it comes with) wide mouth, big lips, pierced tongue or no teeth. The no teeth mouth type was my favorite plus it was the easiest one to clean. You also can tell the doll to place herself in any position you want. It is very flexible that you can put her legs behind her shoulders with her toes touching her lower back; that's how flexible it is. It also is equipped with 5 different modes: Aggressive mode (when it rides you roughly until you cum), Virgin mode (when the doll uses her hands to push you off while you penetrate and tries to push you off during the intercourse while crying), Slave mode (when you tell the doll to do anything you want),

Actress mode (when the doll plays either a teacher, doctor, maid, boss, fitness trainer and many more), Wet dream mode: when the doll signals that you're sleep by hearing you snore (you have to record your snoring and transfer it to the data in the doll for in order it to work) It'll automatically wake out of its sleep and give you a blowjob. Today millions of females around the world are marching and campaigning to get this five thousand dollar love doll off the market and they are fighting for the makers of this doll to stop producing it and to destroy it. I don't get what all the fuss is about, it's just a doll. It is 2016, what is a single guy supposed to do with just his hand and a bottle of lotion? We men don't campaign against women using dildos, so why they are campaigning to get the GS7 2000 Fantasy love doll off the market. Again its 2016, who still uses their hands, and what about the single men. I can't wait til they come out with the GS7 3000 Fantasy love doll. It's an upgrade model that is supposed to be available to the public in the summer of 2017 but unfortunately it was postponed to be release at a later date due to the current campaigning for the removal of the GS7 2000 Fantasy love doll. I was so souped for this doll because of the added features such as the replaceable ethnic head (which means it comes with a black, white, Asian, Indian and Latina head). It also has an upgraded orgasm system where you can pick the intensity of her orgasm which means whether you want her to cum a lot or a lil. You can set the time you want her to cum and she will cum on your penis. The makers also added training modes such as: pull out mode (where it trains you to pull-out at an expected time) and longtiviety mode where the doll trains you to hold your nut for an extended time. Too bad I probably

have to wait for 2018 to get this doll
or might have to get it in another
country.

Do you feel guilty watching porn?

It's natural for men to choose
younger women because young
represents new, fresh, beauty and full
of energy. The NBA always looks for a
young talent, The N.F.L loves younger
players and every model agency
chooses younger people over older
people. To win the beauty pageant,
you have to be young. In the
entertainment world, 30's is
considered old. The older you are the

harder is for you to get recognized, especially if you into hip hop. I say that to say this, what is the difference to men choosing their escorts? Men who are looking to pay for sex (either because he single or he has an old wife) is automatically looking for a younger woman. Perhaps 18 to 25. They crave those ages in hopes these young women could bring them back to their youth, and of course because young represents beauty. So it doesn't mean a man have pedophilic tendencies because he rather have sexual relations with an 18 year old instead of the 45 year old. My old neighbor who was cheating on his wife with a young woman told me why he would cheat on his wife with an old woman if he already has an old woman at home, when I asked him why she had to be young. The point is we men are being brain washed to believe only young represents beauty when aged is also beauty too but is overlooked. It is because when we look at Hollywood movies, TV shows, porn, model agencies; beauty is represented by young people such as 18 year olds. Porn today is pedophilic. Amateur porn is the most viewed out of all the other categories. All actors on amateur porn is either 17 turning 18 or 18 years old, and 21 years older women posting as 18 year olds. Majority of porn sites has a cartoon or anime category that displays the characters as a child younger or way younger than the legal age. Plus the fact that the characters moans in a child's voice makes it secretly a child porn category. Does any adult who watches amateur porn or anime porn has pedophile tendencies? There's another category that represents child porn that's available on all porn sites and those are "school sex' where teachers pretend to have their students come into detention and they are disciplined by sexual favors, WTF! How is this viewable when there are really teachers out there that take advantage of students. Another category is "babysitters" where men fuck their young babysitters. It surprises me that none of the babysitters are nannies. Speaking of more pedophile tendencies; porn displays another category called "cheerleaders" and they are not talking about professional nor college cheerleaders. These cheerleaders pretend to be high schoolers. Who runs these porn sites? How are they able to be posting secretly child porn? But a man like me could go to jail for paying for sex. Luckily I never did but the longer I stay single, the higher my chances are getting caught. I like young punani but not inexperience punani; I usually go for 21 and older. Any girl younger is considered taking advantage unless we shared the same IQ. I'm not going to try to fight to get this type of porn removed but to raise awareness of our morality. But they want to arrest a man that try to turn his fantasy into reality after they show these videos to fantasize. When god destroyed Sodom; it was because of the sexual things Americans are doing today.

Should Prostitution be legal?

My thought is that since porn is legal to watch and participate, then prostitution should be legal also. Pornography is basically prostitution because actors get paid to have sex. The only difference between porn and prostitution is that porn is recorded and prostitution isn't. The directors of porn are the same as pimps of a prostitute. Because of the porn actors are being directed, it is not real sex. Same goes for prostitution because the prostitutes rushes their clients or directs their clients on where to cum. Any man that dealt with prostitution before knows that they're done after they cum. Real sex doesn't finish after a man cums. Real sex isn't timed or limited. The prostitute is there to get a quick dollar and the client is there to get a quick nut. 99% of prostitutes rush their clients because secretly they don't really enjoy it after a couple of clients have came through. A prostitute who loves their job is not a prostitute, she's a whore. Any prostitute that prostituted herself more than 2 years is a whore. A woman who sells herself to get out of a predicament to get on their feet is not a whore, but a hustler. Like a drug dealer who sell drugs more than 5 years is a dumb ass, not a hustler. Unless we all had equal opportunity, none of us should judge one another but help one another. Some people grow up without parenting, without financial stability, and without knowing from right and wrong, so instead of judging a female prostitute, we should help her get out of it. If she was able to start her own business through prostitution, then she wasn't being a prostitute, she was pimping those men. Sadly some of these prostitutes been selling their body for 5 years and still didn't make any progression. It has a lot to do with mismanagement of money. A prostitute should be able to make enough money in a year to get herself out of prostitution. But drugs like mollies, weed and alcohol or whatever they use to stay high to hide the shame of their occupation, keeps them being a prostitute. If they stop spending all their money on those drugs, then they can save themselves out of that lifestyle. I don't recommend that lifestyle but eventually some women will fall victim to it, so I suggest they avoid pimps and drugs if they want to hustle their way out of it. If I was a female who happens to fall rock bottom, I would use my punani to get out that situation too. The good thing is that we are allowed to sin but as long you don't keep sinning or enjoy your sin, then you should be alright with God. A prostitute had came in the room and washed Jesus feet and she was forgiven. So should prostitution should be legal? Why not, porn is. Porn being legal to make and watch is hypocritical when prostitution isn't. They both carry the same risks.

Sorry No Black Men!!!

The next paragraph is off subject but it's just something I want to explain before I go

I know many of you guys (if you're black) that looked for prostitutes on Backpage saw an ad posted by black women, white women, Latina women and Asian women that says "Sorry no black men". At first I thought it was a racist thing until I saw black women posting that sign as well, and then I knew it was more to the story. When I dealt with escorts, I popped the question, why do you women always post ads

44

that says no black men; and they all replied with the same answer (they had a bad experience with black men). Now I was puzzled because I didn't know what their definition of experience was for they never told me what happened so all I could think of that the black men that they serviced for didn't pay them. Me being curious, I searched around on google and YouTube to find my answer. After collecting a bunch of resources, I find out most of these escorts believe black men are cheap, disrespectful and maybe will rob them. It does have some truth to it because just about every month we see/hear reports about Craiglist and Backpage escorts and clients being robbed and it always black men being the robbers. I didn't believe it until I was robbed, being set up by a fake ad. I thought I was going to get some punani but surprisingly when a gun was put to my head, I turned into a punani myself. I happened to be in Newark, NJ. I promised myself to never deal with Newark escorts ever again. Then I started to pay more attention and was able to spot the fakes on Craiglist and Backpage. White folks post fake ads too but their ads (which usually have one pic) ask you to verify your name by signing up to their website so they can trust you enough to talk to them on the phone. Basically their ad is to promote a dating website. The fake ads hosted by black people only intentions is to rob you. Robberies been going on so much from Backpage and Craiglist I had to stopped going on there and rather masturbate. So now I was clear to why escorts say no to black men. And to add the fact that when I use to enter the motels where I met the escort, a host of black men hung around the motel balconies and grounds voiding the discreet of people privacy. I used to be so embarrassed because I was hoping I didn't know anybody and nobody didn't know me. I couldn't understand why these black men hung around the motels and be loud at that. It's like they were proudly open about thirsting for hookers by whispering at them every time one of them walk by. When I realize you couldn't be discreet around black men, then I understood why the escorts say no to black men. There might be other reasons but that was my reason that I have witnessed. I love my brothers but they messed it up for all the single black men who are trying to be discreet about getting a simple nut. Another theory of why they say no to black men is because of the perception of the client. Most these girls think of themselves as "upscale" to some degree to lure in more white guys for bigger bucks. "No blacks" is just a quality stamp on their advertisement that's designed to attract white men who supposedly have a lot of money. This is a trend that's taking over Backpage that sooner or later single black men will have to buy a love doll if he wants a quick nut. My personal own theory to why escorts say "sorry no black me" was that if they let a black man screw them, they will be out of business for a while because of the perception of us having the biggest pipes. I used to think that these escorts rather have a host of average penises throughout their working hours so that they can recover by the next day. But if they screw a black man, they won't recover in time to make enough money to even pay for their room. This has to be a part of the reason, because now there are more ads that say "I love Asian men". When I started to see that type of ad more than "I love white men" I figured that it has something to do with penis size. The smaller the penis size the more they can endure. The more Asian clients, the more clients they can get. One black client equals one client. Another theory is, black men will try to get the lowest cost to screw and non-black males will pay more for nothing. For instance, a white man will pay big bucks to a hooker just to play with herself, while a black man wants everything in the package for the lowest price. To conclude this, it has nothing to do with race as I believe. It has nothing to do with race but everything to do with money. If It has everything to do with pleasure and nothing to do with money then these escorts will most likely say "no to Asians and white men" or "I prefer black men". Once we black men realize that these hookers are only seeking bigger bucks not pleasure then they'll erase their "sorry no black guys" ads.

Other books by this author

Painting the walls of the streets black